Scotland's Kings and Queens

Barbara Mure Rasmusen

First published in Great Britain by Heinemann Library
Halley Court, Jordan Hill, Oxford OX2 8EJ
a division of Reed Educational and Professional Publishing Ltd

OXFORD FLORENCE PRAGUE MADRID ATHENS
MELBOURNE AUCKLAND KUALA LUMPUR SINGAPORE TOKYO
IBADAN NAIROBI KAMPALA JOHANNESBURG GABORONE
PORTSMOUTH NH (USA) CHICAGO MEXICO CITY SAO PAULO

Printed in China

00 99 98 97 96
10 9 8 7 6 5 4 3 2 1

ISBN 0 431 07872 6

British Library Cataloguing in Publication Data
Rasmusen, Barbara
Scotland's kings and queens. – (Scottish history topics)
1. Scotland – Kings and rulers – Biography – Juvenile literature 2. Scotland –
History – Juvenile literature
I. Title
941.1'00992

Acknowledgements
The Publishers would like to thank the following for permission to reproduce photographs:

Ancient Art and Architecture Collection: p.7 right; His Grace the Duke of Atholl's Collection,
Blair Castle: p.20 bottom; John Bethell: p.6 top; British Library: p.7 top left, p.12 left, p.14 top;
The Master and Fellows of Corpus Christi College: p.11 top; Robert Harding Picture Library:
p.13 left; Mansell Collection: p.21 top; National Galleries of Scotland: p.14 below, p.15, p.17
right; National Maritime Museum, Greenwich: p.20 top; National Museum of Antiquities:
pp.4-5 top; National Trust: pp.16–17 centre; Pitkin Pictorials Ltd: p.10 bottom; Public Record
Office: pp.18–19 top centre; Royal Collection, St James's Palace, © Her Majesty The Queen:
p.10 top right, p.16 left, p.18 left and bottom, p.19 top right; The Duke of Roxburghe: pp.8-9
centre; Kenneth Scowen: p.8 left.

Cover photograph reproduced with permission of The Duke Roxburghe, Floors Castle.

Our thanks to Meg Lorimer of Burgh Primary School, Galashiels, for her comments in the
preparation of this book.

Every effort has been made to contact copyright holders of any material reproduced in this
book. Any omissions will be rectified in subsequent printings if notice is given to the
Publisher.

Contents

The making of the kingdom
 (AD843–1058)   4

Malcolm III (1058–93)   6

The House of Canmore
 (1093–1165)   8

The House of Canmore
 (1165–1290)   10

The House of Bruce (1306–71)   12

The House of Stewart
 (1371–1460)   14

The House of Stewart
 (1460–1542)   16

Mary Queen of Scots (1542–67)   18

James VI (1567–1603)   20

Glossary   22

Timeline   23

Index   24

The making of the kingdom (AD 843–1058)

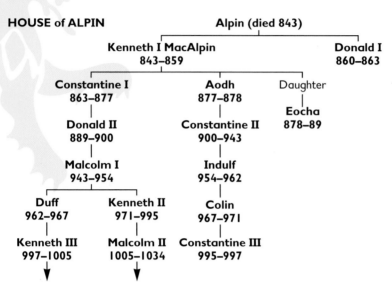

HOUSE of ALPIN   Alpin (died 843)

- Kenneth I MacAlpin
  843–859
  - Constantine I
    863–877
    - Donald II
      889–900
      - Malcolm I
        943–954
        - Duff
          962–967
          - Kenneth III
            997–1005
        - Kenneth II
          971–995
          - Malcolm II
            1005–1034
  - Aodh
    877–878
    - Constantine II
      900–943
      - Indulf
        954–962
        - Colin
          967–971
          - Constantine III
            995–997
  - Daughter
    - Eocha
      878–89
- Donald I
  860–863

ABOVE:
This carving was found on t wall which the Romans buil from the Forth to the Clyde in AD 142. It was built 'so that the Picts were pushed back into what was virtually another island'. Written by Tacitus in 'Agricola'.

RIGHT:
An eighth-century Pictish cross.

The three kingdoms

In AD 843 Scotland was divided into several kingdoms. The kingdom of the Picts was the land north of the Forth and Clyde valleys. The Scots kingdom was in Argyll. The Britons ruled over Strathclyde.

War between the Scots and Picts

At first the Scots and Picts lived in peace. But then they began to fight about who should be king of the Scots, Picts and Britons. In AD 843 Alpin, king of the Scots, was at war with the Picts. Most of the Scots were killed and Alpin was captured and **beheaded**. His son, Kenneth MacAlpin, became the next king of the Scots. He wanted to attack the Picts at once. His chiefs refused to fight, no matter what he said.

Kenneth made a plan. One night he gathered all his chiefs together. When they were asleep he dressed one of his relatives in a robe of shining silver fish scales.

The Rights to Succession – Picts and Scots
Picts   When the Picts came to Britain, only a few women came. The Picts made an agreement with the Irish Scots. The Picts could marry the Irish Scottish women, but could not **inherit** any land or the kingdom. Only the women could do that.
Scots   The Scots chose an **heir** to the throne, usually male, while the king was still alive. The heir was called *tanaiste rig*, which means 'second to the king'.

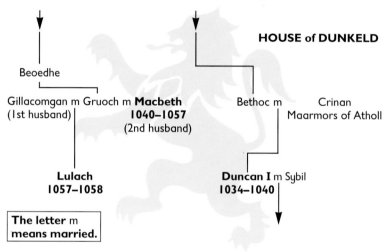

HOUSE of DUNKELD

Beoedhe

Gillacomgan m Gruoch m **Macbeth**   Bethoc m   Crinan
(1st husband)   **1040–1057**   Maarmors of Atholl
   (2nd husband)

Lulach   **Duncan I** m Sybil
1057–1058   **1034–1040**

The letter m means married.

The shining man told the chiefs that they should obey their king and fight the Picts. The next morning all the chiefs could talk about was the angel who had appeared during the night. They agreed to fight. More Scots came from Ireland. They all fought fiercely. They killed the Pictish **warriors**. They went on killing until many Pictish men, women and children were dead. The Pictish king Drasco was caught and beheaded. This is how Kenneth MacAlpin became the king of the Scots and Picts.

One kingdom
Kenneth's **descendants** ruled over the two countries until 1018. Then Malcolm II won the lands as far south as the River Tweed. In 1034 Kenneth's grandson, Duncan I, who ruled over the Britons in Strathclyde, became king. The three kingdoms became one – the kingdom of Scotland.

Malcolm III (1058–93)

LEFT:
Edinburgh Castle.
In 1093, as Queen
Margaret lay dying
here, news was
brought of the death
of her husband,
Malcolm III, and
their son, Edward.
They had been
killed at Alnwick
Castle in England
during a **siege**.
'A certain soldier
brought to Malcolm
III the keys of the
castle on the point
of a spear, put the
king off his guard
and slew him.'

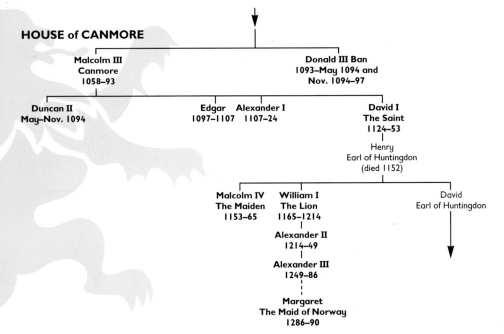

HOUSE of CANMORE

Malcolm III
Canmore
1058–93

Donald III Ban
1093–May 1094 and
Nov. 1094–97

Duncan II
May–Nov. 1094

Edgar **Alexander I**
1097–1107 1107–24

David I
The Saint
1124–53

Henry
Earl of Huntingdon
(died 1152)

Malcolm IV
The Maiden
1153–65

William I
The Lion
1165–1214

David
Earl of Huntingdon

Alexander II
1214–49

Alexander III
1249–86

Margaret
The Maid of Norway
1286–90

Duncan I (1034–40) was killed in battle by Macbeth who became the next king of Scotland in 1040. Duncan's sons Malcolm III and Donald Ban had to leave Scotland. Malcolm III went to England. He lived there for fifteen years. When Macbeth and his Scottish **council** of **nobles** began to disagree, Malcolm III was asked to come back to Scotland. He fought and killed Macbeth at Lumphanan in 1057. He also killed Macbeth's stepson, Lulach, a few months after he had been crowned king by Macbeth's supporters. In 1058 Malcolm III was crowned King of Scotland at Scone. He ruled for 35 years. His son and **heir**, Duncan II, was born to his first wife, Ingibjorg.

Queen Margaret

His second wife Margaret, an English princess, tried to make life in Scotland more like life in England. Malcolm III and Margaret had six sons and two daughters: Edward, Edgar, Edmund, Ethelred, Alexander I, David I, Maud and Mary.

ABOVE LEFT:
Queen Margaret was made a saint in 1251 because she was a very good person. She cared for the poor. She built monasteries and encouraged pilgrims to visit Dunfermline **Abbey**.

ABOVE:
St Margaret's Chapel, Edinburgh Castle. Queen Margaret spent a lot of time praying in this chapel.

The House of Canmore (1093–1165)

Edmund and Donald Ban then ruled over Scotland together for the next three years, 1094–97.

ABOVE:
Melrose Abbey. David I built many abbeys: Dryburgh, Kelso, Newbattle, Dundrennan, Holyrood, Jedburgh and Melrose. Melrose Abbey was built in 1144–46 as a memorial to his mother Queen Margaret.

After Malcolm III died, several members of his family ruled over Scotland. His brother, Donald Ban, ruled during 1093–94. Then the English King, William Rufus, helped Malcolm III's son Duncan II to take the throne. He ruled from May until November 1094. He was killed by his stepbrother, Edmund, and his uncle, Donald Ban.

With the help of an English army, Edgar, the fourth son of Malcolm III and Margaret, attacked and defeated them. Edgar then became king. He was known as Edgar the Peaceable (1097–1107). He kept the peace in Scotland by giving more freedom to the Norsemen, the Anglo-Saxons and the Scots.

When Edgar died, his brother Alexander I (1107–24) became king. The Maarmors (leaders) of Ross and Morne made a surprise attack on Alexander I. He escaped and gathered a large army. He defeated the Maarmors. He then began to take back some of the freedom which his brother Edgar had given. Alexander I died in 1124.

ABOVE:
*The great seal of Alexander II, great-grandson of David I. This seal was used on **documents** belonging to him.*

Malcolm III's sixth son, David I (1124–53), now became king. He had been brought up in the English court. He made many changes. He brought many Norman knights with him from England. He gave them land in return for their promise of **loyalty**. He made new laws, and encouraged trade between towns and with other countries. He built many **abbeys**. He brought order to Scotland. When he died his grandson, Malcolm IV (1153–65), came to the throne.

LEFT:
This drawing shows David I and his grandson, Malcolm IV. David I was a very religious man. He did not drink too often or eat too much. He treated everyone equally and fairly. Malcolm IV was crowned king in 1153 at the age of fourteen. He had to fight with Sumerled of Argyll, Angus of Galloway and with the men of Moray to keep his kingdom. He died in Jedburgh at the age of 26. He was buried in Dunfermline Abbey.

The House of Canmore (1165–1290)

RIGHT:

Alexander III paid **homage** *to Edward I for the lands he owned in England. This picture shows him at the English Parliament.*

Malcolm IV to William the Lion

Malcolm IV reigned for twelve years (1153–65). He never married and when he died his brother William became king. He was known as the Lion. He ruled over Scotland for 49 years (1165–1214). William was captured by the English at the **siege** of Alnwick in 1174.

He had to sign a treaty with Henry II, King of England, before he was set free. He had to become a **vassal** of the English king. He had to allow English soldiers to take over four Scottish castles. He had to send his brother, David, as a hostage to England. When Henry II died in 1189, William paid 10,000 marks to make Scotland **independent** again.

ABOVE:

John Balliol kneels before Edward I in 1292. Balliol rebelled in 1296.

The Golden Age (1214–86)

The reigns of Alexander II (1214–49) and Alexander III (1249–86) were known as the Golden Age. There were no real wars. Many **abbeys**, churches and castles were built. Most of the countryside was **cultivated**. No goods were **exported** from the country during Alexander II's reign, so there was plenty for the people to eat. More castles and churches were built. Alexander III was killed in an accident in 1286. His grand-daughter, Margaret, who lived in Norway, was to become queen. She died of sea sickness in 1290 while on her way to Scotland.

John Balliol (1292–96)

John Balliol was chosen to be the next king of Scotland by Edward I of England, in 1292. He was a king without any real power and Edward I removed him from the throne in 1296.

HOUSE of BALLIOL

David
Earl of Huntington

Margaret m   Alan
(died 1228) Lord of Galloway

Devorguilla m John Balliol
(died 1290)

John (Balliol) m Isobel
1292–96
(died 1313)

Edward (Balliol)
Aug.–Dec. 1332, and for periods
during 1333–46 (died 1363)

ABOVE LEFT:
Alexander III
crowned at Scone.

The House of Bruce (1306–71)

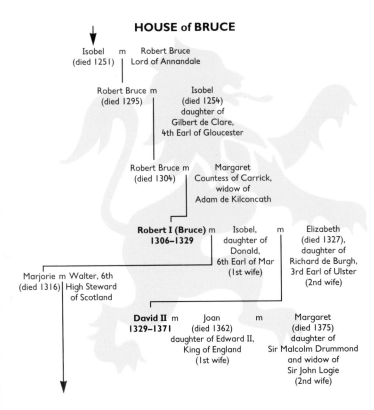

HOUSE of BRUCE

Isobel m Robert Bruce
(died 1251) Lord of Annandale

Robert Bruce m Isobel
(died 1295) (died 1254)
daughter of
Gilbert de Clare,
4th Earl of Gloucester

Robert Bruce m Margaret
(died 1304) Countess of Carrick,
widow of
Adam de Kilconcath

Robert I (Bruce) m Isobel, m Elizabeth
1306–1329 daughter of (died 1327),
Donald, daughter of
6th Earl of Mar Richard de Burgh,
(1st wife) 3rd Earl of Ulster
(2nd wife)

Marjorie m Walter, 6th
(died 1316) High Steward
of Scotland

David II m Joan m Margaret
1329–1371 (died 1362) (died 1375)
daughter of Edward II, daughter of
King of England Sir Malcolm Drummond
(1st wife) and widow of
Sir John Logie
(2nd wife)

Interregnum – a time between kings (1296–1306)

The Scottish people had no king or queen from 1296 to 1306. During these years Edward I of England attacked Scotland. His men captured all the castles. English **sheriffs** and **baillies** ruled over the countryside. Many people were killed or imprisoned. At last in 1297 Sir William Wallace became the leader of the Scots. He and his soldiers fought bravely against the English. Then in 1305 he was captured and killed by order of Edward I.

ABOVE:
During his reign David II was a prisoner in England for eleven years (1346–57).

The House of Bruce (1306–71)

Robert the Bruce and John Comyn, who could both claim the right to rule Scotland, now became the **Guardians** of Scotland. They did not like the way the Scots were being treated. They made a pact. Robert the Bruce would try to become king of Scotland while John Comyn would get all the land belonging to Bruce. John Comyn, however, betrayed Bruce to Edward I of England. When Bruce found this out, in 1306, he arranged to meet Comyn in Greyfriars Church in Dumfries. A fight began and Bruce killed Comyn inside the church. He knew that there was only one thing he could do. He had to claim the Scottish throne or be an **outlaw** for the rest of his life. Bruce was crowned King of Scotland at Scone in 1306. His long struggle to free Scotland began.

By 1313 only Stirling Castle was occupied by an English **garrison**. Sir Philip Mowbray, the keeper of the castle, said he would give the castle to Bruce if the English king, now Edward II, did not come to Stirling by Midsummer's Day 1314. Edward II came with a huge army. The small Scottish army defeated them at Bannockburn on 24 June 1314.

Bruce kept on fighting for Scotland's freedom until 1327 when Edward III, the new English king, signed a **peace treaty**. War with England was over.

When Bruce died in 1329 his young son, David II, became king. Edward Balliol, John Balliol's son, tried to take the throne of Scotland from him twice but he did not succeed. David II died without an **heir** in 1371.

LEFT:
The statue of Robert the Bruce at Bannockburn. He chose the battlefield, prepared the ground and led his men into battle.

The House of Stewart (1371–1460)

RIGHT:
James I, who fell in love with his wife, Lady Joan Beaufort, at first sight. He wrote about it in his famous poem 'The King's Quair'.

TOP:
James I ruled in Scotland for thirteen years. He gathered his nobles together to a parliament each year to make new laws.

ABOVE:
James II was known as 'James of the Fiery Face' because he had a birthmark on one side of his face.

Robert II (1371–90) was the grandson of Robert the Bruce. He was 54 years old when he became king. He had two wives and many children. When he died in 1390 his eldest son John, Earl of Carrick, became the next king. He was crowned as Robert III. This was because the name John was thought to bring bad luck.

Robert III was a very tall man with a snow-white beard. He had been kicked by a horse and was so badly injured that he could not ride into battle with his men. His brother Robert, Duke of Albany, had more control over the Scottish **nobles** than he had. When Robert III's son David died in a **suspicious** way, he sent his son James I to England for safety. James I (1406–37) was only twelve years old when Robert III died in 1406. He was kept prisoner in England until he was 30. A **ransom** of 60,000 marks was then paid and he returned to Scotland.

James I made many changes to life in Scotland. Some of the Scottish nobles were angry at the new taxes they had to pay. A group of nobles, led by Sir Robert Graham, burst into James I's **bedchamber** in Perth and stabbed him to death in 1437.

His son James II (1437–60) was only six years old. Scotland was ruled over by two **chamberlains**, Crichton and Livingston, until James II was old enough to rule by himself. In 1460 James II was taking part in a **siege** at Roxburgh when a **cannon** exploded and killed him.

HOUSE of STEWART

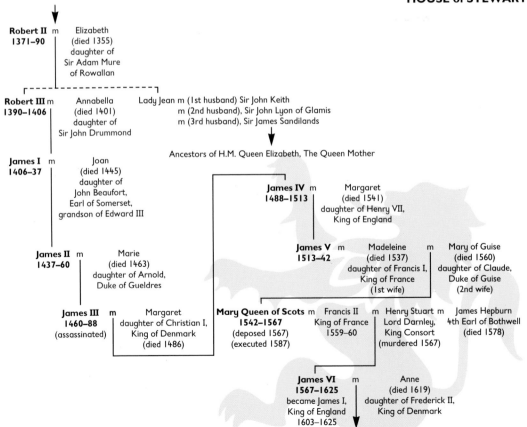

Robert II m Elizabeth
1371–90 (died 1355)
daughter of
Sir Adam Mure
of Rowallan

Robert III m Annabella   Lady Jean m (1st husband) Sir John Keith
1390–1406 (died 1401)   m (2nd husband), Sir John Lyon of Glamis
daughter of   m (3rd husband), Sir James Sandilands
Sir John Drummond

Ancestors of H.M. Queen Elizabeth, The Queen Mother

James I m Joan
1406–37 (died 1445)
daughter of
John Beaufort,
Earl of Somerset,
grandson of Edward III

James IV m Margaret
1488–1513 (died 1541)
daughter of Henry VII,
King of England

James II m Marie
1437–60 (died 1463)
daughter of Arnold,
Duke of Gueldres

James V m Madeleine m Mary of Guise
1513–42 (died 1537) (died 1560)
daughter of Francis I, daughter of Claude,
King of France Duke of Guise
(1st wife) (2nd wife)

James III m Margaret
1460–88 daughter of Christian I,
(assassinated) King of Denmark
(died 1486)

Mary Queen of Scots m Francis II m Henry Stuart m James Hepburn
1542–1567 King of France Lord Darnley, 4th Earl of Bothwell
(deposed 1567) 1559–60 King Consort (died 1578)
(executed 1587) (murdered 1567)

James VI m Anne
1567–1625 (died 1619)
became James I, daughter of Frederick II,
King of England King of Denmark
1603–1625

The House of Stewart
(1460–1542)

James II's son, James III (1460–88), was more interested in science, medicine, **astrology**, poetry and music than he was in ruling the kingdom. The **nobles** and the people of Scotland began to dislike and distrust him. His two brothers **plotted** against him. One of them, the Duke of Albany, led an English army against him, but even then James III remained king. At last many of the nobles rebelled. The rebels, led by James III's eldest son, James IV, fought and won a battle at Sauchieburn in June 1488. James III was killed after the battle.

LEFT:
James V and Mary of Guise, his second wife. James V found out what was really happening in his kingdom by travelling around the countryside disguised as a farmer. The people recognized him, however, and called him the Gudeman o'Ballengeich.

The new king, James IV (1488–1513), was well liked by all his people. He made sure that the Scottish nobles **educated** their sons. A large warship was built and soldiers were trained to use **cannons**.

ABOVE:
James IV. 'He is of noble stature, neither short nor tall and as handsome in complexion and shape as a man can be ... He is active and works hard ... He is courageous ... He is much loved.' – written in 1498 by Don Pedro de Ayala.

FAR LEFT:
This picture painted in 1476 shows James III, his son James IV and St Andrew, patron saint of Scotland.

In 1503 James IV married Margaret Tudor, sister of Henry VIII of England, and a **peace treaty** between England and Scotland was signed. When Henry VIII attacked France in 1513, James IV broke the treaty and marched with an army into England. There, at Flodden Field, he was killed.

James IV's one-year-old son, James V (1513–42), was now king. Over the next fourteen years the country was governed by several people. James V began to rule the country alone when he was sixteen. By that time he had learned not to trust the Scottish nobles. He took advice from the **clergymen** instead and became a very strong supporter of the Catholic Church. The Scottish nobles expected James V to listen to them, but he did not.

When England and Scotland went to war once more in 1542, the nobles were not willing to fight. The Scots army was defeated at the Battle of Solway Moss. James V died at Falkland a few weeks later.

Mary Queen of Scots
(1542–67)

ABOVE:
Mary was very beautiful. She was tall and slender with hazel eyes.

RIGHT:
This pendant was made for Darnley's mother, the Countess of Lennox, to remind her of Lord Darnley and his father.

A tragic Queen

Mary Queen of Scots became queen in 1542 when she was six days old. She was taken to France when she was five. In 1558, at the age of sixteen, she married the Dauphin Francis, son of the King of France. He died two years later. Mary then returned to Scotland. In 1565 she married her cousin, Lord Darnley.

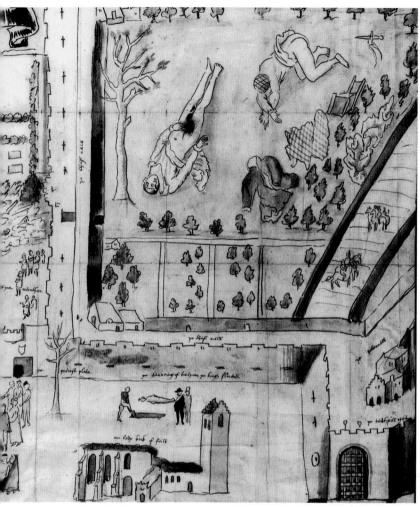

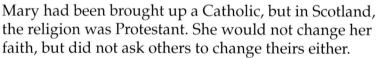

Mary had been brought up a Catholic, but in Scotland, the religion was Protestant. She would not change her faith, but did not ask others to change theirs either.

After the birth of Mary and Darnley's son, James VI, in 1566, Darnley was murdered. Mary married the Earl of Bothwell in 1567. Mary and Bothwell were accused of planning Darnley's death. Mary was imprisoned in Lochleven Castle. She managed to escape and went to England. She was imprisoned there for nineteen years. She **plotted** unsuccessfully with Catholic noblemen to kill Queen Elizabeth I of England. This led to her trial and execution in 1587.

James VI
(1567–1603)

The Union of the Crowns

James VI was born on 19 June 1566 and crowned king on 19 July 1567. His mother, Mary Queen of Scots, escaped to England in 1568 and he never saw her again. Until 1578, Scotland was ruled by his regents – Moray, Lennox, Mar and Morton.
James lived in Stirling Castle with his tutor George Buchanan until he was fourteen.

ABOVE:
James VI of Scotland believed in the 'divine right of kings'. This meant everyone had to do as he told them. He could do what he liked.

LEFT:
This picture shows Mary Queen of Scots and her son, James VI, standing side by side. Two pictures were copied in 1583 to make this one.

George Buchanan **educated** James well. He taught him to speak Latin, Greek and Hebrew by the time he was eight. He taught him astronomy, history, geography and to write poetry. The Scottish **nobles** watched the young king. He was once kidnapped by a group of them because they were afraid he might change his religion from Protestant to Catholic. James VI was **heir** to Queen Elizabeth I of England. When she died in 1603, he went to England with his wife, Ann, to claim the throne. He was crowned in Westminster Abbey in 1603 and became King of Scotland and England until his death in 1625.

ABOVE:
James VI of Scotland, also James I of England, sitting in Parliament in London. Queen Elizabeth I named him as her successor when she lay dying.

Glossary

abbey – a monastery or a convent

astrology – the study of the way the positions of the moon and stars affect human behaviour

baillie – a person who makes sure everyone keeps the peace

bedchamber – a bedroom

behead – to kill someone by cutting off their head

cannon – a large gun

chamberlain – a person who looks after a king's house and money

clergyman – a member of a church who takes a religious service

council – a group of people who meet to discuss plans

cultivated – ploughed or dug over

descendants – children or grandchildren

documents – papers that have information written on them

educate – to provide teaching or training

embroidery – a design or picture on cloth made using a needle and thread

export – to sell goods to a foreign country

garrison – a group of soldiers living in a castle in order to defend it

guardian – a person who guards, protects or defends

heir – a person who gets the title and belongings of a relative who dies

homage – promise to obey

independent – ruling alone

inherit – to receive a title or money from another person

interregnum – a time between the reign of one king or queen and the next

loyal – faithful to a person or idea

noble – a person who has a title e.g. a lord

outlaw – a person who is not protected by the laws of the land, usually because he or she has broken the laws

peace treaty – an agreement made to stop a war

plot – a secret plan

ransom – the release of a person or property in return for another person or money

sheriff – someone who makes sure that everyone keeps the law

siege – to surround a castle or city, not allowing anyone to leave or enter, in order to capture it

succession – following one behind the other

suspicious – questionable

tragic – sad

vassal – one who has to obey

warriors – men who fight

Timeline Kings and Queens of Scotland

843–59	Kenneth MacAlpin, first King of Scotand
860–63	Donald I, brother of Kenneth MacAlpin
863–77	Constantine I, son of Kenneth MacAlpin
877–78	Aodh, son of Kenneth MacAlpin
878–89	Eocha, cousin of Aodh
889–900	Donald II, son of Constantine I
900–43	Constantine II, son of Aodh
943–54	Malcolm I, son of Donald II
954–62	Indulf, son of Constantine II
962–67	Duff, son of Malcolm I
967–71	Colin, son of Indulf
971–95	Kenneth II, son of Malcolm I
995–97	Constantine III, son of Colin
997–1005	Kenneth III, son of Duff
1005–34	Malcolm II, son of Kenneth III
1034–40	Duncan I, grandson of Malcolm II
1040–57	Macbeth, grandson of Malcolm II
1057–58	Lulach, grandson of Kenneth III
1058–93	Malcolm III, son of Duncan I
1093–94	Donald Ban, son of Duncan I
1094	Duncan II, son of Malcolm III
1094–97	Donald Ban, Edmund step brother to Duncan II
1097–1107	Edgar, son of Malcolm III
1107–24	Alexander I, son of Malcolm III
1124–1153	David I, son of Malcolm III
1153–65	Malcolm IV, grandson of David I.
1165–1214	William I, grandson of David I
1214–49	Alexander II, son of William I
1249–86	Alexander III, son of Alexander II
1286–90	Margaret, Maid of Norway, granddaughter of Alexander III
1292–96	John Balliol, second cousin to Margaret
1306–29	Robert I (The Bruce), second cousin to Margaret
1329–71	David II, son of Robert the Bruce
1371–90	Robert II, grandson of Robert the Bruce
1390–1406	Robert III, son of Robert II
1406–37	James I, son of Robert III
1437–60	James II, son of James I
1460–88	James III, son of James II
1488–1513	James IV, son of James III
1513–42	James V, son of James IV
1542–67	Mary Queen of Scots, daughter of James V
1567–1603	James VI, son of Mary Queen of Scots (died 1625)